"Good Morning My Lovilies"

Vol. I

Inspiration Affirmation Of Peace Blessings Love And Light

LOLITA LOUISE RICHARD

To order additional copies of this book, contact:
Xlibris
844-714-8691
www.Xlibris.com
Orders@Xlibris.com

ISBN: Softcover   978-1-6641-1950-5
         EBook   978-1-6641-1923-9

Print information available on the last page.

Rev. date: 09/04/2020

"GOD IS ENOUGH FOR ME. I AM ENOUGH, GLORIOUS AND WONDERFULLY MADE. I AM GRATEFULLY BLESSED AND SO IT IS ASE".

- Lolita Louise Richard

Special Dedication

Robyn (Ronnie) D. Beck The Breaking Chainz Project

Patti Mars- Campazon

Michelle L. Hill- Black Sunflower

Latasha Grant- Pretty Young Bosses

Lesa Lewis- Diamonds Project

Angie Maldonado- Angies Organix

Jennifer Gilbert- J Gilbert Ministries

Dedication

This Book Is Dedicated To:

My Adorable Family And Friends

Who Have Loved Me, Taught Me, Supported Me, And Shown Me Unconditional Kindness And, Patience Thank You...

- llr

Agnes C. Newman	Karen Colton
Paul E. Newman	Becky Turner
Joann Pettus-Mays	Valerie Milligan Rochon
Cora Pettus	De'siree Quintana
Nicholas Newman	Camille Stanley
Juan C Newman	Joshua Haynes
Carlos Pettus	Barbara Haynes
Marquita Pettus	Tom Haynes
Pamela D. Richard	Tina Baggett

Timothy M. Richard

Penny Richard

Joanna M. Richard Mattison

Larry L. Richard

Deborah D. Washington

Maurine Norris

Lee Boone Nwaje'

Dee Becket

Nova Johnson

Rosetta Smith (BFF)

Mandy Reynolds

Meeka Smith

Ruth Dreher

Anthony Jesse

Phillip Caldwell Sr.

Angel Goode

Carol Harris (CJ)

Debra Brown

Janae Carrol (BFF)

Kendra Carrol

Michael Reyes

Fabiola Garcia

Karen Mitchell

Veronica Singh

Brenda Kelly

Eilyon Dye Rather

Torrey Esalomi

Jonathan Davis

Jonetta Whitten-Smith

Juill Jones

Kaylan Jonson

Cindy Little

Lee Harris

Jojo Jaques

Pia M Daniels

Julie Davoe

Jason Seales

Antonio Washington

Ciara Wright

Carlos Strong

Delita L. Newman

Campazon Family

Kansas Family

Tennesse Family

Florida Family

Texas Family

Missouri Family

Look Inside...

1. GOD
2. BLESSINGS
3. STRENGTH
4. LOVE
5.LIGHT
6. JOY
7. PEACE
8. HOPE

viii

God

GOOD MORNING MY LOVILIES
MY COMPLETE TRUST IS IN GOD
THAT'S IN ME AND IN MYSELF PERIODT
I KNOW WHO I AM

…llr 2020

GOOD MORNING MY LOVELIES
LET'S GRACIOUSLY SEEK THE LOVE
OF GOD FOR OURSELVES AND THE
GREATER GOOD OF ALL

…llr 2020

GOOD MORNING MY LOVILIES
WE SHOULD BE COLLABORATING
WITH GOD
FOR OUR OWN ALIGNMENT

…llr 2020

GOOD MORNING MY LOVILIES
DEAR GOD USE ME TO SHINE MY LIGHT
SO OTHERS MAY FIND THEIRS

...llr 2020

Blessings

GOOD MORNING MY LOVELIES
WE MUST CARE FOR OURSELVES
BEFORE TAKING CARE OF OTHERS
WHO CARE FOR NO ONE

…llr 2020

GOOD MORNING MY LOVILIES
I AM SO BLESSED
AND SO GRATEFUL FOR ALL
THAT I HAVE
AND EVEN IF I HAD NOTHING AT ALL

…llr 2020

GOOD MORNING MY LOVELIES
WE EXIST IN THIS PARADIGM
FOR OUR SOULS
PURPOSE STAY MINDFUL

…llr 2020

GOOD MORNING MY LOVILIES
WE ARE ABUNDANTLY BLESSED ALWAYS FOR
BEING BLESSINGS EACH DAY FOR THOSE IN NEED

...llr 2020

Strength

GOOD MORNING MY LOVILIES
WE ARE ALL IN THIS TOGETHER
LET US VIBRATE COLLECTIVELY
AND SPIRAL UP UP AND AWAY FROM
GRIEF AND DISPARITY

…llr 2020

GOOD MORNING MY LOVELIES
WE PUT OFF UNTIL TOMORROW
WHEN TOMORROW MAY NEVER COME
STAY IN THIS PRESENCE
MANIFEST FOR THE HERE AND NOW

…llr 2020

GOOD MORNING MY LOVILIES
WHAT GLORIOUS POWER
WE POSSESS WHEN WE STEP INTO
OUR OWN POWER, WHEW

…llr 2020

Love

GOOD MORNING MY LOVILIES
I'M LOVING THE ME
THAT I'M BECOMING
EACH DAY AND I STILL
HAVE ENOUGH LOVE TO
LOVE THE YOU THAT YOU ARE

…llr 2020

GOOD MORNING MY LOVILIES
LISTEN LOVELY ONES
FEEL OUR FEELINGS
THAT WAY WE KNOW
WHAT WE CAN HANDLE

…llr 2020

GOOD MORNING MY LOVILIES
OUR IMPACT OF LOVE TOUCHES,
REACHES, CLARIFIES
EMPOWERS MUCH MORE
THAN ANY IMPULSE OF HATE

…llr 2020

GOOD MORNING MY LOVILIES
I'M GOING TO LOVE EVERYTHING I LOVE
WITH ALL THE LOVE I HAVE WITHIN ME
YES INCLUDING YOU

...llr 2020

Light

GOOD MORNING MY LOVELIES
WE ARE THE THREAD IN THE FABRIC
OF OUR EXISTENCE THAT
HOLDS US COMPLETELY INTACT

…llr 2020

GOOD MORNING MY LOVILIES
I WILL HONOR THE DAY AND SHINE
MY LIGHT IN EVERY DARK CREVICE

…llr 2020

GOOD MORNING MY LOVILIES
EVERYDAY I STRIVE
TO BE THE GOOD NEWS
I'M WAITING TO HEAR
EVEN IF I HAVE TO BE THE MESSENGER

…llr 2020

Joy

GOOD MORNING MY LOVILIES
IN JOYOUS LAUGHTER
LOVE LIGHT AND FOND REMEMBRANCE
OF WHO WE ARE
WE MOVE FORWARD

…llr 2020

GOOD MORNING MY LOVILIES
THIS IS OUR LIFE
TO DO THAT WHICH
GIVES US JOY

…llr 2020

GOOD MORNING MY LOVILIES
WHAT WONDROUS JOY WE ENCOUNTER WHEN
WE INSPIRE UPLIFT ENCOURAGE OTHERS IN
OUR OWN PURSUIT OF HAPPINESS AND
PEACE

..llr 2020

Peace

GOOD MORNING MY LOVELIES
WE MUST TEACH OURSELVES TO BE
COMFORTABLE AS MUCH IN PEACE
AS WE ARE IN WAR

…llr 2020

GOOD MORNING MY LOVILIES
MAY WE FIND GENUINE PEACE
IN THOSE
THINGS WE SEEK FOR HAPPINESS

…llr 2020

GOOD MORNING MY LOVILIES
THERE IS POWER AND PEACE IN KNOWING
ACCEPTING UNDERSTANDING OUR SOLE
PURPOSE FOR US BEING HERE IS TO
SERVE

...llr 2020

Hope

GOOD MORNING MY LOVELIES
DEAR BEAUTIFUL ONES
WE ARE NO LONGER WAITING
ON OUR DESTINY
OUR DESTINY HAS BEEN
WAITING FOR US TO SHOW UP

…llr 2020

GOOD MORNING MY LOVELIES
LET'S ANTICIPATE
OUR NEXT MOVES
IN CASE OUR LAST ONES
FALLS THROUGH

…llr 2020

GOOD MORNING MY LOVELIES
NO MATTER WHERE I AM
I'M ALWAYS RIGHT HERE FOR YOU

…llr 2020

Printed in the United States
By Bookmasters